C000175022

Tombland, Norwich

In and
NORWICH
THEN and NOW

Philip Standley

Photography
Terry Burchell

John Nickalls Publications

Previous Titles (Philip Standley)
Norwich in Old Picture Postcards Volumes 1, 2, 3 and 4
Norwich Then and Now

First published in 2002 by John Nickalls Publications
Oak Farm Bungalow, Sawyers Lane, Suton,
Wymondham, Norfolk, NR18 9SH
Telephone/Fax: 01953 601893

ISBN 1 904136 09 5

DEDICATION
Dedicated with love to my wife Mary, my son Paul,
my grandson Miles and especially to my daughter Sarah
who helped me research and write this book
as I have now been diagnosed with Parkinson's Disease.

Printed by Geo. R. Reeve Ltd
9-11 Town Green, Wymondham,
Norfolk, NR18 0BD
Telephone: 01953 602297

INTRODUCTION

For this book we were kindly loaned the use of an album of pre-1900 photographs, clearly showing the tremendous differences to life in Norwich in those days. This was a time and way of life which will never return. This period of change began when the new tram system of 1900 created new roads, which we now take for granted as we drive or walk through the city. The city's claim in 1939 was that: "There is a pub for every day of the year and a church for every Sunday", whilst seventy years previously it is believed there was at least two pubs for every day of the year. What would today's figures be? Whilst many have closed, many still survive and new nightclubs and bars have appeared across the city.

Norwich then suffered terrible damage in the bombing raids of World War Two and especially in the 'Blitz' of April 1942. Despite Hitler's plan, the people of Norwich proudly came through and the post-war years saw more change to the face of the city with redevelopment and clearance of historic buildings at the hands of the planners. In hindsight, some of these changes have not always been for the better. But time marches on and new developments are always under construction. For example, Riverside is still expanding and work has now commenced on demolishing the old Nestlé factory site for redevelopment. There is even talk of reinstating the tramlines or a similar system. Time will only reveal if this ever comes into operation.

This book is not intended to be a definitive history of Norwich and District, but just an informal glance at the changes encountered over the years and we trust our readers will enjoy our selection as much as we have putting it all together. We hope our great grandparents would still be proud of the city and next time you are out in Norwich, please just stop, look and remember its history and appreciate it for the fine city it is.

Philip Standley September 2002

FRONT COVER: Pull's Ferry *Norwich – Then and Now*
TITLE PAGE: Tombland *Norwich – Then and Now*
BACK COVER: The Royal Arcade
ABBREVIATIONS: c (circa) – approximate; *pu* – postally used ; p.h. – Public House

FOREWORD

Good grief! Look at that! Would you believe it! Some of the images in this book of the way it was and the way it is now are quite shocking. Looking back we should ask ourselves: "How on earth did they get away with it?"

It is easy to criticise now but at the time planners were trying to turn ancient Norwich, with its twisty and narrow roads, into a city that could cope with traffic. In some cases it worked. In others it was a disaster. Whole streets changed beyond all recognition and many fine buildings were pulled down.

But we can't blame the planners for every incident of civic vandalism.

The Luftwaffe finished off the work by destroying large parts of Norwich in the Blitz of 1942. Today the city continues to change shape with the huge and controversial redevelopment schemes at Riverside and on the former Nestlé chocolate factory site at Chapelfield.

Last year author, historian and postcard collector Philip Standley and photographer Terry Burchell teamed up to produce *Norwich – Then and Now* which was a smash hit.

They hit on a simple idea. Select an old postcard and then take a photograph from exactly the same view and compare the two.

The public loved it and demanded volume two – so here it is and this time it includes some of the views in villages surrounding Norwich.

It is a fascinating book. An intriguing look at the way things have changed over the years. Sometimes for the better.

Anyone interested in Norwich and Norfolk will love it. I did and would like to congratulate Philip and Terry. Planners of the 21st century would do well to keep a copy by their side.

Derek James – *Features Editor, Evening News, Norwich*

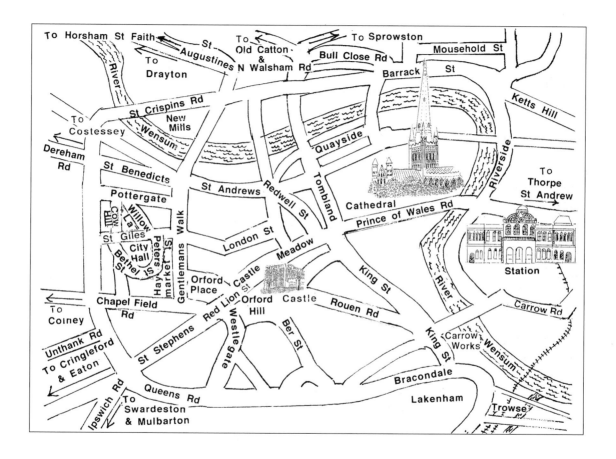

THEN – THE HOME & COLONIAL STORES LIMITED, 18 ST STEPHEN'S STREET *c*1912: A fine example of the Home & Colonial's shop front, complete with an impressive name sign, fretwork and lamp to welcome you to their shop.

The manager and his staff in their long aprons photographed on a typically damp Norwich day, proudly stand by the displays of their selection of groceries for sale including 'Perfect' margarine and 'H & C Pure Cocoa'.

In Norwich at this time there were also Home & Colonial Stores at 16 St Benedict's Street and 2 Brigg Street.

RHODA BUNN COLLECTION

NOW: Following the German bombing raids of the Second World War, many factories, shops and homes were reduced to burnt-out shells. Here on St Stephen's Street, this was one of these areas which suffered severe damage, particularly in the Baedeker raids of April 1942. They were known as this after Baedeker's *Guide to Britain*, a German publication listing places in England of great historic interest, which the Luftwaffe then decided to deliberately bomb. Nos. 14–18 St Stephen's Street were rebuilt in the post-war years in its present-day style. The site of the old grocers store is now the entrance to Pearl Assurance House, which is currently the home of First National Bank Ltd.

THEN – THE PEACOCK PUBLIC HOUSE, ST STEPHEN'S PLAIN, c. LATE 1890s: The Peacock dated back to 1760 and the brewers of the ales served were Young's, Crawshay & Young's. On the far left can be seen the Coach and Horses, a Morgan's public house dating back to 1802. How many of us would recognise this view today, especially with the fully-laden horse-drawn cart outside Mrs Sarah Dawson's newsagents. All these buildings would soon disappear. *RHODA BUNN COLLECTION*

NOW: Nothing of the old view remains as this whole length of Red Lion Street was set further back when it was redeveloped, widening the road for the tram lines. Barclays Bank now occupies the premises on the left. Next door, the Coach and Horses remained open in its new premises until 1984. It is currently a Pizza and Pasta restaurant. Across Peacock Yard, The Peacock closed its doors in 1958 and was later demolished. Ladies' fashion chain Evans today occupies the site.

41 *NORWICH. — Westlegate Street. — LL.*   Sel. cta

THEN – WESTLEGATE: 1912 records reveal that the rector of All Saints' Church, standing at the top of Westlegate, was the Rev Johnstone Murray MA. Services were held at 8am each Sunday with evensong on alternate Sundays at 7pm. Following restoration of the tower in 1913 the ring of three bells was increased to five.

Richard Ransome, bootmaker, was located at No. 8 Westlegate, whilst the thatched gable building with the handcart was occupied by Arthur Kemp, greengrocer.

In the 19th Century this had been the Light Dragoon public house and was more commonly known throughout Norwich as the 'Barking Dickey'. Folklore says the pub sign more resembled a badly painted braying donkey than the intended Lighthorseman's steed. With 'dickey' being Norfolk dialect for donkey, the 'Barking Dickey' was so named and never forgotten amongst locals.

NOW: The city street we know today as Red Lion Street was at one time all part of Westlegate. Today, Westlegate is a much busier and widened one-way thoroughfare compared to the quaint, narrow street of the early 20th century. These days All Saints' Church is the 'All Saints' Centre' – as an 'Ecumenical Multi-Purpose Christian Centre' providing a selection of gifts, cards and books as well as a library and coffee shop together with a rest area and chapel. The old 'Barking Dickey' has in its time been a bank but is currently a coffee shop called Casaccio's. The remaining buildings have been flattened to make way for Westlegate House, which houses a branch of the world-famous burger chain, McDonalds.

THEN – RED LION STREET, *c*1898/99: Photographed during preparation for the laying of the tramlines, on the left, the original Orford Arms is in the process of demolition – although they are still serving at the bar! In the distance is the junction with Rampant Horse Back Street, whilst further along the row of shops, on the corner with Little Orford Street, confectioner John Pike had already vacated his premises and moved to Davey Place.   *TERRY NICHOLLS COLLECTION*

NOW: The Orford Arms was relocated in the new premises, Anchor Buildings, designed by George Skipper. It closed its doors on 16 February 1974 to become offices and the Halifax Building Society vacated the premises in the summer of 2002. The sheer magnitude of the introduction of the tram system and post-war redevelopment is clearly visible. Rampant Horse Back Street disappeared with the rebuilding of Curl's Department Store, now Debenhams, whilst Little Orford Street is now Orford Place.

Norwich, Orford Place

THEN – ORFORD PLACE: Confusion over the street names of this area has occurred over the years owing to the arrival of the trams, and the Baedeker raids of World War Two. Following the demolition of the buildings between Rampant Horse Back Street and Little Orford Street, the triangular hub of the tram system – Orford Place – stood on the site. Curl Brothers' Drapery Store is on the left, whilst on the right are the Burlington Buildings, designed by J Owen Bond and built in 1904. *RHODA BUNN COLLECTION*

NOW: In late April 1942, Norwich endured a series of devastating air raids in which 235 people were believed to have died. Much of the city centre was obliterated and became unrecognisable overnight. The burnt-out shell of Curls was cleared to basement level to become a static water tank, holding 270,000 gallons, during the remainder of the war. Prior to the rebuilding of Curls, a surface car park occupied the site. The new department store was vastly enlarged by building on the old tram island.

THEN – ORFORD PLACE, *c*1932: The arrival of the trams made Orford Place one of the main focal points of city life. Here, the No. 13 car on the Unthank Road to Magdalen Road route, is seen with Curls in the background. The first services were launched on 30 July 1900, initially with four routes: Magdalen Road, Earlham Road, Dereham Road and Thorpe Road. Four further routes were added the same year, giving a total of 14.81 route-miles. *BASIL GOWEN COLLECTION*

16

NOW: One would get quite a shock if a tram came rumbling towards you along the narrow, and now pedestrianised, Orford Place. In the mid-1920s, the trams began to receive competition from the 'bus services which had been introduced to cater for the developing outlying areas. Despite improvements to the tram system, the writing was on the wall heralding its demise. In July 1935 the withdrawal of the trams began and the last tram car took its final journey into the Silver Road depot on 10 December 1935.

THEN – WILLIAM A CLARKE, IRONMONGER, ORFORD HILL: Taken in 1898, just prior to its demolition to make way for the direct cut through to Castle Meadow for the tram lines. William Clarke's emporium was a thriving business judging by the variety of goods on display. A visit there must have been quite an experience compared to his modern-day counterparts. Then photography was still a novelty and everyone was happy to pose for the cameraman. *RHODA BUNN COLLECTION*

NOW: How many of us take this familiar view of Norwich Castle for granted, little realising the changes that took place here. Following the loss of Clarke's store for the direct cut for the tram system, the road was raised at the lower end, accounting for the railings and steps down to White Lion Street. On the right the ancient coaching inn, the Bell Inn, is still a thriving part of the nightlife of Norwich, whilst Abbey National also occupy part of the inn, facing Orford Hill.

THEN – YORK TAVERN, 8 CASTLE MEADOW, *c*1898/99: Another example of Norwich's lost past just prior to the arrival of the trams. Photographed from the Bell, with York Alley to the left, the original York Tavern, dating back to the 18th century, would soon be demolished and rebuilt, widening Castle Meadow. Located close to the horse and cattle markets, the bar staff were kept busy on market days. On the far right can just be seen the popular Castle Hotel. *RHODA BUNN COLLECTION*

NOW: The new York Tavern became known as the York Hotel and even today still bears the name 'York House' on one of its pediments. Times were changing again on Castle Meadow with the Cattle Market moving to Hall Road in 1961. The licence of the York Hotel was surrendered on 24 November 1964. Today the premises are occupied by a variety of retail outlets. The Castle Hotel remained until it was demolished to make way for the Castle Mall Development of the 1990s.

THEN – NORWICH LIBRARY: Yards and streets like Lady Lane and Austin's Yard were flattened in the early 1960s to make way for the Bethel Street public car park and the Norwich Central Library which was opened by Queen Elizabeth, the Queen Mother, in 1963. On the morning of 1 August 1994, a plume of smoke rose over the city as the Local Studies, Lending and American Memorial Libraries suffered devastating damage in a disastrous blaze. *DEREK JAMES – EASTERN EVENING NEWS*

NOW: Our comparison photograph is taken about 30 metres closer to St Peter Mancroft than the previous view, due to the sheer size of the new building. Following the devastating fire, plans were drawn up for a new library known as The Forum to be built. It was designed by Sir Michael Hopkins, with the project costing £63.5 million. The impressive Forum, officially opened by Queen Elizabeth II during her Golden Jubilee visit in July 2002, offers a wide range of new libraries and other amenities.

THEN – ST PETER'S STREET: This was a bustling street with the fish and provisions markets both nearby, together with a plentiful supply of stores and inns. St Peter Mancroft, built between 1430 and 1455 in the perpendicular style, is the largest church in Norwich. The row of shops in the distance were demolished in the 1960s to allow for the Bethel Street public car park. The premises on the immediate right were flattened in the 1930s for the new City Hall which opened in 1938.

NOW: St Peter's Street is another example of road widening resulting from the redevelopments over the years. The area by the gates of St Peter Mancroft is used as a motorcycle park these days. St Peter Mancroft still keeps watch over St Peter's Street, Bethel Street and the Haymarket, whilst visitors have been known to mistake this popular church for Norwich Cathedral. The old Bethel Street car park is now the impressive foreground to The Forum.

THEN – BETHEL STREET: On the extreme left is the yard of Lacey & Lincoln Ltd, builders' merchants, a former home of a Victorian skating rink. Next door at No. 36 is the Coachmakers' Arms public house. Nos. 20–36 were all demolished in the spring of 1933 following a compulsory purchase to make way for the new Norwich City Fire Station, whilst work began in 1935 to clear the remainder for the City Hall. On the right Bethel Hospital is shown, founded in 1713. *ERIC READ COLLECTION*

NOW: Photographed from a slightly different angle to reveal the widened Bethel Street we are nowadays familiar with. Country & Eastern now occupy the former builders' merchants with their gallery of oriental rugs and textiles. The new fire station was built by W J Simms Sons & Cooke Ltd of Nottingham and was officially opened by the Lord Mayor of Norwich, Alderman F C Jex, on 9 November 1934. The Forum is visible on the right of the picture and the old Bethel Hospital buildings survive.

THEN – THE PICTURE HOUSE, HAYMARKET: Seen here is the original frontage of the Picture House with 372 seats, opened in February 1911 on the premises of the old London and Provincial Bank. In 1921, the cinema was virtually rebuilt to seat 1,700 cinemagoers, and in 1929 the stage was enlarged and the cinema refurbished for the 'talkies'. The first talking picture shown was 'The Singing Fool' starring Al Jolson on 18 February 1929. *RHODA BUNN COLLECTION*

NOW: The Haymarket Picture House changed its name to the Gaumont in 1955. However, in 1959, the cinema closed in line with the nationwide decline in the film industry. Following demolition in 1961, new shop premises were built. Currently young fashion shops, Top Shop, Top Man and Miss Selfridge occupy the site. Next door, on the right, the George Inn, became known as the St George & Dragon Inn and after closure became a bank. In 2002, a further branch of burger chain McDonald's opened in these premises.

Castle Meadow, Norwich

THEN – CASTLE MEADOW, *pu*1932: At this time the trams were still in use, however the splendid motor cars seen here were becoming more popular amongst affluent city folk. Castle Meadow had been widened during 1926/27 due to the clanking trams almost scraping the railings between the road and Castle Gardens, leading pedestrians to fear they would become trapped. Fletcher's large printing works dominates the view. *RHODA BUNN COLLECTION*

NOW: In recent years, Castle Meadow has become open only to buses and taxis, and available for access only to other vehicles. Despite this, it can still be quite a risk dodging the busy throng of buses. The central road islands have remained in a similar design, even one of the original trees has survived. The old printing works is now called Castle House and a selection of retail outlets occupy the premises, whilst on the right is the new building of Ottakar's book store and coffee bar.

THEN – REDWELL STREET, *c*1898: This view is taken prior to the direct cut through to extend St Andrew's Street to Bank Plain for the route of the new tram lines. The central premises and those to the rear of them were soon to be flattened. On the left is the Cabinet Makers' Arms PH which, in 1900, would become the City Arms' PH following demolition of the old City Arms on the corner of Princes Street. Next to Brady's Yard is furniture dealer, George Bury. *RHODA BUNN COLLECTION*

32

NOW: Following the cut, the broad sweep of St Andrew's Street has now been opened up and the former Festival House public house, now Delaneys, on the corner with St George's Street is visible. George Bury's furniture store is now occupied by the stylish textile and furnishings shop of Country & Eastern. The name of Redwell Street originates from the Red Well, which was located on the corner of St Michael at Plea's churchyard by Queen Street.

THEN – WAGGON & HORSES INN, 17 TOMBLAND: This listed building originates from the fifteenth century and was used by the London carriers. At one time the Waggon & Horses Inn had its own smithy at the rear of the premises. Benjamin Rufus Blomfield became the licensee on 12 May 1896, taking over from Joseph Wilde. He remained there until 24 August 1900, when Mary Ann Blomfield took over the licence.

RHODA BUNN COLLECTION

NOW: The Waggon and Horses remained until the mid-1970s when, after a short closure, the inn reopened in 1976 as the Louis Marchesi and is still known as this today. It was named after the founder of the Round Table, whose first meeting was held in Norwich in 1927, as a society for local business and professional men. Previous brewers here have been Steward & Patteson's and Watney's. Waggon and Horses Lane still exists to the right of the building today.

THEN – QUAYSIDE FROM FYE BRIDGE, *c*1920: The River Wensum had actively played an important part in the wealth of the city for centuries, with a steady flow of cargo vessels commonplace. With the use of the rail system becoming more popular, the river had started to see a decline in its use. The riverside storage buildings on the left have a sheer drop down to the waterside. The tall building on the right was the Municipal School, whilst on the other side of Pigg Lane was the New Star public house.

NOW: By the 1930s the left-hand side of the river had been widened, along with similar projects at Whitefriars Bridge, proving it was not only the streets of Norwich succumbing to widening schemes. Consequently the old buildings on the left were demolished. The school remained empty for several years before becoming an antique centre and has recently been converted into residential accommodation. The New Star was demolished in 1963 and replaced with the current building.

THEN – KETT'S HILL, *c*1912: Taken looking up Kett's Hill, in the area known as Little Spitalfield. Behind the brick wall on the left was the vicarage for St James' Church. At No. 23, Mrs Eliza Ransome's drapery and haberdashery shop is seen. Robert Arthur Elvin was the baker at No. 25, whilst to the right is the Kett's Castle public house owned by Young's, Crawshay and Young's. Next door, divided only by an alley, can just be seen the end wall of the Ostrich Inn, run by Mr Albert Mace.

NOW: The vicarage was demolished in 1938 and is now the site of the busy roundabout we know today, built in 1959. The row of dwellings which included Mrs Ransome's shop have also been demolished. After all those years No. 25 is still a bakery – Kett's Hill Bakery – whilst next door is Paul Kent's Hair Studio. The Kett's Castle p.h. sustained bomb damage in 1942, and is now known as Kett's Tavern. The Ostrich Inn had suffered flood damage in 1912 and was demolished in the 1950s.

THEN – ROBIN HOOD PUBLIC HOUSE, MOUSEHOLD STREET, *c*1910: Folk from the local community gather outside The Robin Hood, not only for the photographer but also to enjoy a spring outing together. Community spirit was rife among these close-knit streets, where people saw each other through good and bad times. The demand for terraced housing was on the increase to house the growing numbers of workers engaged in Norwich's booming trades at this period in time.

NOW: The Robin Hood had originally been situated in Barrack Street in the 1800s, but moved to its present location on the corner of Mousehold Street and Anchor Street when Barrack Street was widened. Generations of people have come and gone, and life on the terraced streets of Norwich will never be the same again but, despite the loss of the old corner shop, The Robin Hood is still serving, now as a freehouse, proving that there is always a place in our hearts for a good old friendly corner pub.

THEN – 106–108 BULL CLOSE ROAD: Established in 1878, Eakson Bliss' business was that of a typical city Sub-Post Office which sold a wide range of goods. He was a baker, a grocer and tea-dealer, both wholesale and retail. On the left is the bread delivery cart, whilst a lady waits patiently on the right in the trap. Again staff and customers proudly stand to be photographed. In Norwich, during 1896, there were thirty Town Sub-Post and Money-Order offices which rose to thirty-five by 1912.

NOW: Here is further evidence of how areas of Norwich have changed beyond all recognition. The old Post Office was demolished when Charlton Road was constructed in the late 1930s. From the same spot today, we see the flats on Charlton Road and beyond is the Barrack Street roundabout, part of the inner link road. The house at No. 104, just visible on the right, is still standing having had its gable rebuilt.

THEN – ST AUGUSTINE'S STREET *c*1905: Photographed near the junctions of Sussex Street and Esdelle Street. On the right-hand side of the street the Catherine Wheel public house can be seen. Among the other establishments, also on the right, are Arthur William Hall, stonemason and Brock Bros, tailors & hatters, where trousers and breeches could be made to measure for 10/6 per pair (52 pence in today's money).

NOW: Not a single horse and cart in sight! These days St Augustine's becomes choked with traffic as it links with Aylsham Road and the Ring Road for Cromer and beyond. St Augustine's has rather suffered since the early 1970s, when the inner link road was built, severing the street from the rest of the mediaeval city and turning it into a busy corridor for motor traffic. The Catherine Wheel is still open, whilst flats are now on the site of the stonemasons and a Dental Practice occupies Brock Bros.

THEN – H J BISHOP, 71 ST AUGUSTINE'S STREET: Boot and shoe dealer Henry Jonas Bishop's premises photographed in the early 1930s. The firm remained for over 60 years, whilst many generations of families were fitted out with new footwear by the staff at this traditional family firm. To the left of Bishop's is St Augustine's Town Sub-Post Office & Stationers, run in 1933 by Miss Ethel Copley. Benjamin Marrison was the hairdresser next door. *TONY WILLIAMSON COLLECTION*

NOW: These days, this is an active junction joining St Augustine's Street, Bakers Road, Aylsham Road, Waterloo Road and Magpie Road, and is controlled by traffic lights. A sign of the times, like many other independent shops, Bishop's sadly closed a few years ago – another well-known name from the past now disappeared from city life. Wensum Properties then moved into the premises and, in March 1997, opened their property management and residential lettings service.

Valentines Series 15567

New Mills at Norwich

THEN – NEW MILLS: Here on New Mills Bridge we see the corn mill of Sharpin & Sons with corn and builders' merchants premises on the left with two wherries moored up. The mill seen here replaced the earlier mills, which were ruined following a dispute with the Abbot of St Benet's in 1440. There had been mills here by the River Wensum since the Norman Conquest. In 1401/2, a survey was commissioned "to examine the place for the new water mills to be built". These were eventually completed by 1430.

NOW: Like many cities of the 1800s, disease was rife in Norwich, with a lack of hygiene and clean water. New waterworks had opened in 1869, but the New Mills' Pumping Station on the site of the corn mills was not built until 1898, creating compressed air to pump the sewage. The pumping station closed in 1974 and restoration followed in the 1990s with the intention of it becoming a museum. Today, the sluices remain in working order, whilst this point of the River Wensum is the limit of navigation.

St. Benedict's Street, Norwich. J 1770.

THEN – ST BENEDICT'S STREET, *pu*1918: St Benedict's had been so densely populated it had four churches along its length; St Lawrence's, St Margaret's, St Swithin's and St Benedict's. Here at the western end of the street, on the left is No. 85, Sarah Baldwin, newsagent; No. 83, Walker's; No.81, Frederick Farrow, butcher and No.79, George Hicks, fishmonger. On the right-hand side William Harvey was the hairdresser, next door was the White Lion p.h. with Fletcher's Confectioners on their left.

NOW: St Benedict's Gates, Barn Road, Grapes Hill and Dereham Road suffered severe damage during the 'Norwich Blitz' of April 1942. Locals discovered an unrecognizable scene of devastation after the raids, as much of the western end of St Benedict's Street was wiped out and many buildings were reduced to rubble and beyond repair. In the post-war redevelopment, St Swithin's Road was built to the left to provide a link with Westwick Street.

Cow Hill & Willow Lane, Norwich. J 8233.

THEN – WILLOW LANE AND COW HILL: Photographed looking up from Pottergate. The gateway on the left led to King's Yard. By taking the left fork to Willow Lane, one will find the house where George Borrow lived. He was the author of *Romany Rye* and *Lavengro* and created the phrase 'Norwich, a fine city'. Behind the crowstepped-gabled house is St Giles' Church, built in the 14th century, and with a tower 120 feet high, is the tallest of the city churches. *BASIL GOWEN COLLECTION*

NOW: St Giles' Church still looks down onto Cow Hill, but the row of old buildings on the left have all been flattened to make way for modern apartments. Many of the other old houses and buildings remain, but Willow Lane now has no vehicular entry from Cow Hill. Whilst the earlier photograph shows not a single form of transport in sight, the street of today is lined with parked cars. The buildings remain much as they were and has thankfully escaped the blitz, bulldozers and city planners.

THEN – 96 ST GILES STREET: The staff of Mr John Edmund Chaplin Sandford's butchers shop proudly stand outside by their display of sides of pork and beef. In those days it was common for butchers to exhibit their wares in this way. Today the health authorities and public would not tolerate these methods of window dressing! Mr Sandford's shop was located at the western end of St Giles Street, just along from the St Giles' Gate Stores public house. *RHODA BUNN COLLECTION*

NOW: On the left, the old alleyway which runs alongside the course of the ancient city walls has survived and now also runs alongside a dual-carriageway! The premises which included the old butchers and St Giles' Gate Stores p.h. were demolished to clear the way for the construction of the inner link road in the early 1970s. This view looks up Grapes Hill to the busy roundabout which serves Cleveland Road, Chapelfield North, Chapelfield Road, Convent Road, Unthank Road and Earlham Road.

"THE TUNS" CORNER, NORWICH, 162. J.H.

THEN – THE TUNS CORNER: Photographed at the junction with St Giles, Chapelfield Road, Unthank/Earlham Roads and Grapes Hill with the overhead tram wires, this is again another view which has undergone changes over the years. Owned by Steward & Patteson's, The Tuns is one of the oldest hostelries in Norwich and had been the scene of political feuds in the 19th century, between its own Tory supporters and the Whigs who frequented the Grapes Hotel opposite. *BASIL GOWEN COLLECTION*

NOW: Due to the widening of Grapes Hill, this is taken from a slightly different angle than the previous image. Again, the skyline and alterations to the surrounding roads have changed the panoramic view. All evidence of the trams has gone. The buildings to the left of The Tuns were demolished and the former Convent of the Little Sisters replaced them. Surviving bomb damage during WW2, The Tuns retained many original features and in 1999 it became the Temple Bar.

THEN – ROSE VALLEY TAVERN, 111 UNTHANK ROAD: Here staff and locals pose for the camera. The lane, Rose Valley, is visible on the right, which at one time had a stone archway with 'Freemans Villas' written on it. The Rose Valley Tavern dates back to the mid-1800s and, at the time of the photograph, James Joseph Deacon was the publican, holding the licence between 1871 and 1902. Lacon's of Great Yarmouth had become the owners in 1894. *RHODA BUNN COLLECTION*

NOW: After more than one hundred years on from the previous photograph, the Rose Valley Tavern is still serving its customers. Now an Adnams of Southwold public house, customers may turn down Rose Valley to park their cars away from the busy Unthank Road. The pub itself has been extended into part of the old living quarters, whilst the frontage has been updated with a bay-fronted window, new doorway and extended right-hand window.

Norwich, Prince of Wales Road

THEN – PRINCE OF WALES ROAD: This had been constructed in the 1860s as a commercial speculation to provide a grand approach to the city from Thorpe Station. The first residential flats in Norwich, Alexandra Mansions, were built here and part of these would later become the Regent Theatre, opened in 1923 and built by The Alexandra Picture House and Theatre Co. Across St Faith's Lane junction is the grand Electric Theatre which opened in 1912, with its own orchestra.

NOW: Today this is one of the most congested streets in the city, especially during the commuter rush. The Regent was acquired by ABC in 1961 and in 1973 tripled its auditorium, and later became the Cannon. In 1995 it reverted back to the ABC Cinema and closed in October 2000, following the opening of new multi-cinema complexes in the city. The Electric Theatre was renamed the Norvic in 1949, but survived only until 1961, and was later demolished with modern offices now standing in its place.

NORWICH.

10782

THEN – ENGINE SHEDS, NORWICH THORPE STATION, *c*1930–1934: Following publication in the Evening News, the engines have been identified as follows: (*left to right*) Class J15 0-6-0, Class B12 express locomotive 4-6-0 No. 8569, Class C12 4-4-2 tank engine, Class B12 express locomotive 4-6-0 No. 8523 and Class J17 0-6-0 No. 8213. The B12s were developed from the famous 'Claud Hamilton' 4-4-0s. A B12 is preserved on the North Norfolk Railway. *BASIL GOWEN COLLECTION*

NOW: Photographed looking towards the city from Carrow Road, the main engine shed seen previously has disappeared to reveal trains still running to the right, with Thorpe Station and the Cathedral visible. The remainder of the site is now a mass of supermarket stores and car parking space on the Riverside Retail Park. The newly-built Koblenz Avenue running behind the centre fence – named after Norwich's twin city in Germany – now links King Street and Carrow Road to Riverside.

EVERARD VESSELS LOADING AND DISCHARGING AT NORWICH, NORFOLK

THEN – RIVERSIDE: An artist's impression of vessels from F T Everard & Sons loading and discharging their cargos. Looking from Carrow Bridge, R J Read's flour mill is seen on the left. In 1932, Robert John Read, Jnr, purchased the derelict buildings of a former yarn mill – the Albion Mill, for £5,750. From here the business flourished as sea-faring vessels could reach the mill and imported grain enabled expansion, whilst Read's Self-Raising Flour became well-known across the country.

NOW: The empty flour mills remain a ghostly reminder that the old days of industry and heavy commercial river traffic have long gone. At present, planning is in process for the site to be redeveloped for flats and housing. The artwork advertising the famous 'Recero Flaked Maize' is still visible on the left-hand wall. Spanning the river is the Novi-Sad Friendship Bridge, opened in November 2001 at a cost of £1.4 million, being one of the more-pleasing aspects of the riverside development.

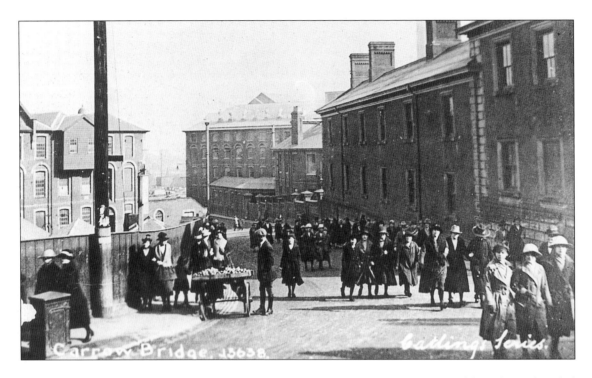

Carrow Bridge. 15638.

THEN – WORKERS LEAVING CARROW WORKS, *c*1918: In 1814 Jeremiah Colman founded his mustard manufacturing business in Stoke Holy Cross. His great-nephew Jeremiah James Colman transferred the firm to Carrow Works in 1854. These new mills had been built to give improved access to rail and river transportation. Colmans grew to become one of the city's largest employers, with some 3,000 employees in the production of mustard, starch, cornflour and the famous Reckitt's Blue Bags.

NOW: Colmans introduced many social reforms; in November 1918, employees with at least one year's service were first given one week's annual holiday. Following a merger in 1938 Colmans became Reckitt and Colman. Today, the company is part of the Unilever Bestfoods UK Group manufacturing mustard, condiments and packet mixes, selling under the brand name 'Colmans of Norwich'. The entrance to the works is now off the County Hall roundabout.

THEN – THE SHIP INN, 168 KING STREET, *c*1930: This is one of the most ancient streets in Norwich and is steeped in history. It was once the most important commercial and residential area in the city. Many wealthy merchants and well-known local families – the Boleyns, Cokes, Howards, Hobarts – resided there in impressive halls and houses. King Street had more pubs than any other street in Norwich. The entrance to Ship Yard is on the left with its beautifully carved lintel, engraved 'Princes In'. It is believed that the Paston family who owned Princes Inn on Princes Street brought this with them when they acquired the property. The 16th century building of the Ship Inn began serving ale in the 18th century and was owned by Young's, Crawshay & Young's at the time of this photograph. The five-gabled flint and brick row of dwellings next door at Nos. 164 and 166 dated back to Elizabethan times.

NOW: The Ship Inn closed on 20 May 1969 and was acquired by the City Council in 1970, and converted into private residences.

In May 1939, a ministry inquiry was held under the 1936 Housing Act to decide the future of Nos. 158–166 King Street. Witnesses described this area as "One of the most historic and architecturally attractive corners left in Norwich" and "Here were some of the best local examples of Dutch influence". Furthermore, Nos. 164 and 166 were detailed as "Elizabethan gabled houses of considerable interest". Despite this opposition, the minister agreed with the City Council and they were all condemned, and demolition followed shortly. The site is now occupied by Matrix Studios and Models Direct.

Today, King Street is a mere shadow of its former self, however there still remains many buildings worthy of note!

Norwich, Thorpe Road, Rosary Corner

THEN – THORPE ROAD, ROSARY CORNER, *c*1920: Tram car No. 13 advances towards the passing-loop by the Stracey Road and Rosary Road junctions on the Thorpe Road route. The sign hanging on the traction column states there is a public telephone here, referring to the Town Sub-Post Office and Chemist's run by Mr Alex Colin Brown on the corner. Thorpe Road was the main route for all traffic travelling towards the East Coast. *BASIL GOWEN COLLECTION*

NOW: The elegant traction column and tram wires have long gone, only to be replaced by the not-so-attractive modern-day street lighting. The splendid terraced houses have withstood the years to create a not too dissimilar view in 2002, however modern office blocks have crept into the distance. Mr Brown's chemist and post office is now 'Le Café Maison'. Following the construction of the Southern Bypass in the early 1990s, much Yarmouth-bound traffic has been taken away from these roads.

Thorpe Village, Norwich

THEN – THORPE ST ANDREW: Seen here is Thorpe Village as you leave Norwich on the Yarmouth Road in the early 1900s. This had become known as Thorpe Narrows amongst locals before the road was widened. In the centre can just be seen the spire of St Andrew's Church rising to 150 feet. The church had been built in 1866, beside the ruins of an earlier church. Thorpe Hall is located behind the right-hand wall where Major Frank Astley Cubitt JP was in residence.

NOW: Residential flats and office space now line the left-hand side of the road. St Andrew's Church spire was damaged during World War Two, resulting in a serious crack and, in 1954, the spire was replaced by a shorter spire. The cottage on the right of the earlier picture remains on the city side of the Town House Restaurant and Hotel, whilst the road to the far right has been named Thorpe Hall Close. The construction of the Southern Bypass has alleviated much of the heavy traffic through Thorpe.

THEN – COLNEY POST OFFICE, *pu1906:* Here the Post Office in the parish of Colney, situated near to the River Yare, on the Norwich to Watton road is photographed. Most small villages had their own post offices in those days. Letters were delivered here from Norwich and despatched twice daily with an early evening despatch on Sundays. The nearest money and telegraph office was at Eaton. On the left was a blacksmith's forge, which was also run by the Sub-Postmaster.

74

NOW: The old post office building is a private house named 'The Old Forge', with the smithy's building having been renovated and now forming part of the main house. The date the house was built is clearly shown inscribed in the brickwork as 1863. The house is situated on Old Watton Road adjacent to the hectic new main road from Watton into Norwich, with the BUPA Hospital, the new Norfolk & Norwich University Hospital and the University of East Anglia close by.

THEN – DEREHAM ROAD: Here is a good example of how the outskirts of Norwich have expanded. This image was taken when Dereham Road was still unsurfaced with only hedgerows, woodlands and gardens lining the cyclists' route. Looking towards Dereham in the early 1900s, the only clue to the exact whereabouts is The Gate House public house. This had previously been the Norwich Gate House where tolls were collected for the Norwich, Swaffham and Mattishall Turnpike.

NOW: There is a sharp contrast between the early 1900's traffic and the congestion of today with the suburbs now continuing for over a further two miles beyond here. The residential areas which have expanded either side of Dereham Road include North Earlham, New Costessey and Bowthorpe. The Gatehouse public house, now surrounded by houses, has been in existence since 1869 and remains to this day. It was rebuilt in 1934 and suffered damage in the April 1942 German Air Raids.

IN WATER LANE. COSSEY. Nᴿ NORWICH

THEN – WATER LANE, COSTESSEY: A posed, but beautiful, photograph taken when the camera was still a novelty. Crossing this ford on the River Tud presented more of a challenge to travellers using Water Lane in those days than today. The previous old rustic bridge had been replaced by this new footbridge in approximately 1907, but it was to be destroyed in the floods of 1912 and subsequently replaced by the first roadbridge, which was built in 1913.

NOW: Today, known as Longwater Lane, it has traffic-calming measures in place for today's vehicles, a contrast to the meandering horses and carts of yesteryear which travelled along here. In 1969, a further new roadbridge was constructed over the old ford, which was diverted under the new bridge. Nowadays, local children enjoy fishing here, or a game of 'pooh sticks' as immortalised by Christopher Robin and Winnie the Pooh.

THEN – DRAYTON STATION: A nostalgic and valuable photograph of Drayton Station on the Norwich City Station to Melton Constable line of the Midland and Great Northern Joint Railway. This was affectionately known as the 'Muddle and Go Nowhere' amongst locals. Here, at Drayton, this short train of open wagons headed by 4-4-0 No. 32 may be waiting in the loop for a passing train. The footbridge was moved after closure to give pedestrians a safer access crossing beside the A1067 road.

NOW: Taken from the same position as the earlier photograph, this most uninspiring image becomes quite amazing when compared with the 'Then' picture. Passenger services closed on this line in 1959, however freight services continued here until the early 1970s. By 1973, eleven thousand wooden sleepers had been lifted from the Norwich to Drayton section of the line and auctioned off. Today, the site of the station has become Drayton Industrial Estate, with the rear of the units seen above.

RED LION, DRAYTON J & S 535

THEN – RED LION, 2 FAKENHAM ROAD, DRAYTON, *pu*1935: Located at the crossroads in the village of Drayton in the vale of the River Wensum, The Red Lion premises dates from 1678, and has been a public house since the 1830s. Charles Walter Neve, previously the publican at the Cock Inn, Drayton, had taken over here in February 1924 and remained until May 1935. Fine examples of transport of the time are seen, with the tourer and double-decker 'bus ready for its return trip to the city.

NOW: The Red Lion was damaged by enemy action in May 1942, but has survived through to the 21st century. Like virtually all public houses today, bar meals are served throughout the day together with the liquid refreshments on offer. There is a new pub sign and the old lean-to on the left is now incorporated in the building. Some of the chimney pots have gone and the entrance and windows have been modernised, whilst an abundance of hanging baskets makes it a very attractive building.

SCHOOL AND SCHOOL HOUSES, SPROWSTON

THEN – SCHOOL LANE, SPROWSTON, *c*1920s: The public elementary school was established by Mrs Arkwright in 1860; John Gurney enlarged it in 1873 and it was expanded again in 1885, 1891 and 1904. It educated both girls and boys, and in 1922 could cater for 460 of them. At this time, Thomas Delves was the master, whilst Miss Lucy Thrower was the infants' mistress. School Lane ran from North Walsham Road, Catton, through to Wroxham Road, Sprowston.

NOW: The school buildings are under the control of Norfolk County Council Education Department as a Training Unit, titled Norfolk Youth Community Services District Resource Base – Broadland. The lovely thatched and timbered house has been demolished and replaced with a modern housing estate on Post Mill Close. School Lane now joins the hectic ring road at Chartwell Road.

THEN – NORTH WALSHAM ROAD, OLD CATTON, *c*1910: Photographed looking northeast at the junction with George Hill and School Lane, a pony and cart makes its way along this part of the old Norwich to North Walsham Turnpike, which had opened in 1797. Mr William Badcock's blacksmith's forge is on the left, whilst The Woodman p.h. can just be seen. This was owned by Young's, Crawshay and Young's and dates back to 1845. Old Catton's Grocery and Provisions Store is on the right.

NOW: Today, the North Walsham Road has become a very busy thoroughfare, as it is the main route to Coltishall and beyond. Traffic lights now control the flow from the four roads. The old blacksmith's premises has become a butcher's shop, whilst the building on the corner with George Hill has been demolished and is now the car-park of The Woodman. The village grocery store has withstood the years and today we are more familiar with National Lottery signs than the previously seen Telephone signs!

THE SWAN ST. FAITH'S. *(Chapman Series.)*

THEN – THE SWAN PUBLIC HOUSE, HORSHAM ST FAITH'S, *pu*1918: In 1912, there were seven inns in the parish of Horsham St Faith's and Newton St Faith's – the Cross Keys, the Crown, the Crown (Newton), the Jolly Butchers, the King's Head, the Swan and the White House. The Swan, seen here with a group of proud soldiers enjoying the sunshine and a mardle, was sold in 1841 by Coltishall Brewery to Steward and Patteson. Joseph Bonnick was the licensee from 1890 to 1924.

NOW: Known as the Black Swan, the premises have still retained many original windows with a few new additional ones together with an elongated canopy and alterations to the chimneys. At the present time it is a Pubmaster outlet and has moved with the times providing satellite television for its patrons. Many of the surrounding buildings and houses have survived, with new properties having been built in between.

THEN – ST FAITH'S UNION WORKHOUSE, *c*1920: The Union of St Faith's was managed by its own Board of Guardians and Officers, and the inmates came from the 29 surrounding villages, which comprised of the Union. The 'Poor Law Institution' was erected in 1805 of red brick, was enlarged in 1849 and 1862, and was capable of accommodating 500 inmates. In 1911, the population of the Poor Law Institution was 6 officials and 75 residents, with the children attending the local school.

NOW: The workhouse closed in 1928 and it is rumoured amongst locals that a laundry was then based on the site. Following the closure, the old workhouse buildings were demolished and the new crematorium, to serve Norwich and Norfolk, was built. This was opened in 1935 and is now known as St Faith's Crematorium. Our photograph shows the chapel which can hold 100 mourners. The crematorium is set in 26 acres of woodland and well cared for Gardens of Remembrance.

THE KING PASSING THROUGH EATON TO NORWICH. OCT 25⊻/09. PIONEER SERIES.

THEN – HM KING EDWARD VII VISIT TO NORWICH, 25 OCTOBER 1909, EATON HILL:
Ladies peek out and gentlemen raise their hats to the King as he passes through Eaton on his visit to the city. In those days this was the main London to Norwich road and the King, seen here travelling in the front car without a numberplate, passed through Attleborough and Wymondham on his way to Norwich and Mousehold Heath where 11,000 schoolchildren had gathered to welcome him.

NOW: Eaton is a busy and popular suburb of Norwich, however the construction of a bypass for the A11 in the 1970s has taken much of the heavier traffic away. This approach to Eaton Street has been altered as it is now the exit road from Newmarket Road leaving the city and it is one-way down to the traffic lights. On the left the Cellar House public house is still there although obscured here by trees, whilst some of the buildings seen on the right of the previous picture have been demolished.

Lamb Inn, Eaton.

THEN – THE LAMB INN, 18 EATON STREET, EATON: This traditionally thatched building first opened as an alehouse in 1760, with James Forster as the licensee. It is recorded that, in 1772, the 'annual Ass and Pig Race' was to be held here with the 'best of three heats from the Lambe to Mile End and back', where the winning ass would be entitled to a 'grand Morocco saddle'. The Lamb was owned by Steward & Patteson's and closed on 29 January 1910 under the Compensation Act.

NOW: Following the closure of the Lamb, the premises were subsequently sold. Today, the building still bears a lovely thatched roof. On the same spot as where the pub sign stood is now the village sign for Eaton. It was presented to the village in 1956 and had been carved by Harry Carter, who designed and carved over 150 village and town signs in Norfolk. Several years ago the building was converted to a bank and is currently a branch of HSBC.

Red Lion, Eaton.

THEN – RED LION PUBLIC HOUSE, 52 EATON STREET, EATON: A tranquil scene of life in the parish of Eaton at the turn of the 20th century, looking towards Norwich, with young lads walking and cycling down Eaton Street and men, mothers and children carrying on with their daily life. The Red Lion, a coaching inn built in the late 17th century and known in the 19th century as the Lion, was owned by Norwich brewers Steward & Patteson's.

NOW: The telegraph poles have gone, the road has been widened and many of the buildings visible previously in the distance have now disappeared, but if you were to walk down the middle of Eaton Street today you would be risking life and limb. The Red Lion remains in business, whilst its impressive dutch gables have stood the test of time. A traffic light system has been installed at the busy junction with Bluebell Road and Church Lane to control the stream of traffic.

THEN – CRINGLEFORD MILL: A beautiful study of Cringleford Mill, on the banks of the River Yare, taken in the early 20th century when Robert John Watling was the miller. Cringleford Mill is mentioned in the Domesday Book, as 'one of the oldest water-mills in the country'. In 1580, the whole village including the mill was destroyed by fire and the mill was rebuilt the following year. The mill and house suffered much damage from the floods of August 1912. *MRS RALPHS COLLECTION*

NOW: In 1916, Cringleford Mill was destroyed by fire. Boy Scouts assisted with the rescue of Mr Watling's family from the burning buildings. The fire was alleged to have been started by strangers seen in the vicinity the previous day. Rumours were rife that the firestarters were German spies! Only the mill house and outbuildings survived the fire. The Watling family restored the mill house which remains today as a private residence in a very scenic setting by the River Yare.

THEN – TROWSE STATION, *pu*1909: Trowse Station has had a varied career; it was originally opened as a temporary terminus until the construction of the swing bridge at Thorpe was completed, with the first train travelling through the station in December 1845. The station is seen here looking towards Thorpe from the bridge, with the sidings on the left and rows of cattle pens on each side indicative of the volume of livestock which travelled to and from Norwich Market.

NOW: Trowse Station closed in 1916 and reopened in 1919. It then closed to passenger traffic for the alleged final time on 5 September 1939. After the war, the station remained a busy cattle and freight depot, however, in March 1986 and February 1987, the station reopened briefly for passengers, due to track improvements and bridge replacement at Thorpe. Passenger trains still travel past where canopied platforms once stood. The goods yards are still in use for the conveyance of stone aggregates.

THEN – THE COCK INN, LAKENHAM, 1908: On the night of 31 March 1908, a fire started at Lakenham Mill, situated at the foot of Long John Hill, across the bridge from The Cock inn. By the time the fire brigade reached the mill it had been destroyed. Sparks from this blaze were blown by a strong wind, igniting the thatched roof of The Cock inn and the adjacent house. Steward & Patteson's of the Pockthorpe Brewery, Barrack Street, Norwich, owned the inn at this time.

NOW: Following the disastrous events of the spring of 1908 when it was said that the flames could be seen from Norwich Market Place, The Cock inn, close to the River Yare, was rebuilt and is still serving a selection of cask ales, hot meals and has a riverside beer garden to enjoy on a sunny day in this village style location on the outskirts of the city. The building now has a porch and an extension looking out over the river and wildlife.

THE "KING OF PRUSSIA" IPSWICH ROAD. NORWICH.

THEN – THE KING OF PRUSSIA PUBLIC HOUSE, IPSWICH ROAD, *pu*1914: Following the outbreak of the First World War, the name was changed to the King George IV for patriotic reasons. Steward & Patteson's owned the premises, whilst Mr John Barrett was the landlord here between 1884 and 1934. This view was photographed at the old junction of Ipswich Road and Hall Road, which was later closed when Hall Road was diverted to a new junction near the Holiday Inn.

NOW: In 1993, the King George IV had another change of name to 'Cactus Jak's' which closed in 1999. In October 2001, Norwich City planners gave the go-ahead to demolish the existing structure to make way for a new public house to be built for the Vintage Inns chain. Demolition started in November 2001 and was completed in January 2002. The 'Marsh Harrier' then opened as a restaurant in the summer of 2002. Today, the volume of traffic here is a sharp contrast to that of 1914.

THEN – TURNPIKE ROAD, SWARDESTON, *pu*1909: The Norwich to New Buckenham turnpike route passing through Swardeston dated back to 1772. The Dog, a Bullard's public house, dated back to 1836. In 1850 the inn had been advertised as an "Excellent public inn with stables, convenient outbuildings, extensive well-planted orchard, garden and a good yard", when sold following the death of its first owner. Morter's General Hardware & Supply Store supplied the village with their groceries.

NOW: The Dog became known as Bowlers between 1996 and 1997, before reopening briefly as the Dog in November 1997, but by 2000 the premises had become Chester's Seafood Restaurant. Swardeston is well known for being the home of Nurse Edith Cavell, where her father was the Vicar. Based in Brussels during the Great War she nursed men from both sides, before being captured and executed on 12 October 1915 by the Germans for assisting in the escape of Allied servicemen.

MULBARTON BRIDGE

THEN – MULBARTON BRIDGE, *pu***1912:** This lovely rural scene was photographed by Tom Nokes of Norwich, who travelled around Norfolk on his bicycle with his camera. In the centre is the Tradesman's Arms Beer House and Bowling Green which dated back to the early 1800s. Records from 1883 show that Mrs Charlotte West Dye was wheelwright, carpenter and beer retailer here. By 1912, Edward Dye is recorded as builder, timber merchant, wheelwright and beer retailer.

NOW: Mulbarton has still retained its pleasant village setting, although the population has obviously increased over the years. In 1962, 143 barrels of beer were sold in the year at the Tradesman's Arms, but it closed its doors on 27 January 1969. The premises, and those of the adjacent buildings on the left, were demolished and residential houses built on the site. Like all our 21st century images this has been taken by Tom Nokes' modern-day counterpart, Terry Burchell, in Terry's home village.

THE SCHOOL, MULBARTON.

MIDDLETON'S SERIES.

THEN – THE SCHOOL, MULBARTON, *pu*1914: School children pose for the camera outside their village school, overlooking the picturesque Mulbarton Common, which covered 47½ acres. The Public Elementary School had been erected in 1865 and enlarged in 1887. In 1912, it could accommodate 120 boys and girls, whilst the average attendance was 91 children. The master of the school, at that time, was Mr Walter Joseph Simmonds.

NOW: Mulbarton First and Middle Schools are now located in more modern buildings further round the Common. The old school building still stands and is a Dental Surgery. Upon closer inspection, one sees that the lovely large window on the end has been converted into two smaller ones. The doorway is where the old chimney breast stood, whilst the old entrance with the bell tower has been bricked up and is now a window. Next door, an extension has been built which houses a pharmacy.

ABOUT THE AUTHOR

Philip Standley was born in Wymondham and has lived there all his life. He spent his working life in the family's hardware and television retail business. The shop had traded for over a hundred years until Philip and his sister Pamela retired in 1988. His main hobby is collecting old picture postcards of Wymondham and Norwich, amongst many others, and he was a founder-member of the Norfolk Postcard Club. His first book *Norwich in Old Picture Postcards* was published in 1988 and was followed by a further three volumes. He also assisted in the production of two books on local railways and last year *Norwich – Then and Now* reached the book shelves.

ABOUT THE PHOTOGRAPHER

Terry Burchell was born in Kent and has lived in Norfolk on and off for thirty-seven years, working mainly in the printing industry and finally as a print ordering officer with HMSO before his retirement. He has been involved in photography for as long as he could hold a camera, both as an amateur and later as a freelance professional. Much of the work he undertakes now is for museums and libraries, copying old photographs and documents.

ACKNOWLEDGMENTS

When I was asked by Steve Benz in 1988 to write *Norwich – A Portrait in Old Picture Postcards, Volume One*, I didn't think that fourteen years later I would be writing number two in our *Norwich – Then and Now* series. Following a marvellous response, my publisher John Nickalls asked if Terry and I would do this further edition. We are indebted to Matthew Williams who kindly provided us with exact locations for the 'now' photographs, as well as all who have loaned postcards and photographs: Rhoda Bunn, Basil Gowen, Derek James (EEN), Terry Nicholls, Mrs Ralphs, Eric Read and Tony Williamson. Special thanks to Ann Hoare for her map artwork, to Ashley Gray for his assistance with the typesetting and layout, to Derek McDonald and Richard Bristow for information on the public houses of Norwich and Norfolk, and Richard Bartram, Mark Hannaford-Dagless, John Stroud and Philip Yaxley for additional information, and to those who wrote to the Eastern Evening News with railway details. Apologies to anyone I may have unintentionally forgotten to include, and should anyone have any old photographs or postcards I would always be interested to see them.